Punch

Drinks to Make Friends With

Shaun Byrne & Nick Tesar

Hardie Grant

BOOKS

Contents

Spirit, sugar, lemon, water and spice:

these are the five components of a punch.

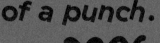

They balance strong, sweet, sour and weak.

Punch is a long cocktail with eye-catching appeal. Its presentation often grabs attention and provokes conversation. But, for us, the best thing about punch is that it's a communal affair. Wherever groups of friends, old and new, gather in celebration, you'll usually find punch. And sharing flavours with friends is one of life's greatest pleasures. Funnily enough, according to bartending folklore, it's considered bad luck to serve yourself punch, so share the love around and serve each other.

Flavours also have the wonderful ability to transport you to a particular time and place based on your memories and experiences. We've written this book with just that in mind. In these pages you'll find punches that whisk you away to the streets of Hanoi with flavours of pho, and transport you to the banks of the Thames to watch the Henley Royal Regatta with friends. There's a punch to evoke the colour and noise of Rio's Carnival, and one to keep you warm while you walk the banks of Melbourne's Yarra River on your way to the AFL Grand Final.

Punch around the world

~~~

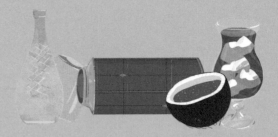

Punch has been around since the 17th century and is said to have been created by workers of the British East India Trading Company. Since then, recipes have evolved as the idea has travelled around the world.

Punch in the Caribbean is different depending on the location. In Barbados it could be based on a little recipe ditty: 'One of sour, two of sweet, three of strong and four of weak'. In Martinique refreshing Ti' punch is served, bringing together Rhum agricole, lime pieces, soda and sugar cubes.

In the US punch can vary widely on the alcohol spectrum. At one end you have the Hawaiian Punch, a tropical juice with zero alcohol. At the other is the Fish House Punch – one of America's first punches – which is laden with rum, cognac and peach brandy, and served with a little lemon juice, sugar and water.

Britain, particularly the Scottish Isles, is thought to be home to the famous Milk Punch from which eggnog evolved. This dairy punch uses citrus to both split and clarify the milk, which made it shelf-stable in the time before refrigeration.

In England punch will commonly feature tea as the spice. Historically wine was used as the base, and most English punches are lavishly garnished with both fruit and vegetables. The English are also famous for their 'cups', such as the Pimm's Cup, which are served at social events.

In Sweden *punsch* is liqueur with an Arrack base, spiced with cinnamon, tea and sugar. It can be served hot or cold.

Wine-based punches can be varied too. *Gluhwein* in Germany is served warm and includes citrus and heavy spices, not dissimilar in flavour to the Spanish sangria, which is served over ice with lots of citrus and fruit.

Just about every culture has its own version of punch. Our love of exploring different places through their culinary landscape and experimenting with local flavours has inspired the recipes in this book.

Using this book

~~~

You need to prepare for punch; it's not as easy as whipping up a gin and tonic or opening a beer. To aid in this, we have broken each of the recipes down into three sections: ingredients, preparation and, of course, serving and decorating. There are different levels of preparation needed; some recipes require you to soak ingredients well in advance, while others are as simple as blending and enjoying.

This book includes a selection of both no- and low-alcohol punches too, so you can remember the event as well as live it in the moment. This is also about catering for everyone. Personal choice, health and sustainability all come into play with alcohol, and we believe that no one should be left out. Look for the 🜄 icon to find recipes that contain little or no alcohol.

Also look for the icons opposite to see recommended serving and drinking vessels, and the best time to enjoy your punch.

Lastly, all punches make 1.5 litres (51 fl oz/6 cups) unless otherwise specified, which is a perfect amount for six people. You can scale any of the drinks up or down based on how many friends you're sharing with.

Key
~~~

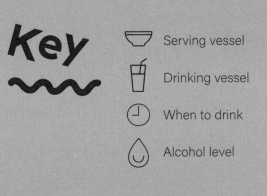

Serving vessel

Drinking vessel

When to drink

Alcohol level

Europe

Strawberry Pimm's slushie

In the English town of Henley on the River Thames, thousands of people come together each year for the summer spectacle that is the Royal Regatta: a rowing festival that lasts for five days. People camp in neighbouring fields and congregate for a very English picnic of sandwiches and Pimm's (a classical fruit cup drink). This recipe is for those wanting to make the occasion extra special.

2 punnets of strawberries
500 ml (17 fl oz/2 cups)
   lemonade (lemon soda)
500 ml (17 fl oz/2 cups)
   ginger ale
bunch of mint
1 cucumber
500 ml (17 fl oz/2 cups) Pimm's

To prep Begin at least 24 hours before serving. Hull the strawberries and blitz to a purée in a food processor. Combine with lemonade and ginger ale. Freeze into ice cubes. For garnish pick the mint sprigs from the stems and refrigerate, ready to serve. Slice the cucumber into discs and refrigerate, ready to serve.

To serve Put the ice cubes into a hand ice crusher and crush directly into your picnic cups. Top with Pimm's and garnish with cucumber slices and mint sprigs.

Tip: Don't get too close to the edge of the river after a few of these; you might fall in.

 Hand ice crusher

Picnic cups

During the Royal Regatta on the banks of the Thames, or at any other English sporting event during their two-week summer!

New wine punch

Beaujolais is a wine region at the southern tip of Burgundy, and it is well known for its production of Gamay. To celebrate the end of vintage, winemakers often put aside their nouveau (the first wine picked, fermented and bottled) to drink when harvest is over and all of the year's ferments are underway. This falls on the third Thursday in November, at the height of Europe's autumnal fruit season. It's a time of year when quinces are ripe, and picnics with friends and family are prevalent.

25 g (1 oz) hazelnuts, roughly chopped
100 g (3½ oz) quince paste
25 g (1 oz) honey
5 g (⅛ oz) salt
750 ml (25½ fl oz/3 cups) Beaujolais nouveau (or other fresh and light red wine)
1 small saucisson, to serve
large wedge of Époisses de Bourgogne (washed-rind cheese), to serve
1 small baguette, to serve

To prep Begin at least 24 hours before serving. Dry-roast the hazelnuts in a frying pan until toasted. Add the quince paste, honey, salt and 1.5 litres (51 fl oz/6 cups) hot water. Stir to dissolve and simmer for 15 minutes over a low heat. Strain and refrigerate to cool. Combine with the wine, stir well and bottle into a magnum. Refrigerate until ready to serve.

To serve Serve the chilled magnum of wine with the meat, cheese and bread. A very rustic affair.

Tip: For an extra layer of texture, pour the prepared wine into a soda siphon and carbonate before serving.

 Magnum

Wine glasses

 After vintage, once all the ferments are on

Low alcohol

Oktoberfest

200 g (7 oz) apricot jam
100 g (3½ oz) pretzels (see tip)
5 g (⅛ oz) salt
700 ml (23½ fl oz) dark beer
150 ml (5 fl oz) orange curaçao

Oktoberfest is the world's largest beer festival, held each year in Munich. Running for the last couple of weeks of September and the first week of October, tourists and locals alike gather in massive beer halls to sing, dance, eat pork knuckles and pretzels, and dress in traditional attire – but, mostly, to drink local beers. This punch brings all of these flavours together.

To prep Begin at least 4 hours before serving. Combine the jam, pretzels and salt with 1 litre (34 fl oz/4 cups) hot water. Blitz in a food processor until smooth. Pour into a saucepan and simmer over a low heat for 15 minutes to make a syrup. Strain through a piece of muslin (cheesecloth) and refrigerate until ready to use.

To serve Pour the prepared syrup into your yard glass, then carefully add the beer and curaçao. Gently stir to combine.

Tip: Buy extra pretzels for serving on the side.

 Yard glass

Pony (liqueur) glasses

Whenever a pork knuckle is on the table – which, during Oktoberfest, is often

The spice trade

The Netherlands has historically been an international hub for the spice trade. While Rotterdam is now the busiest port in Europe, Amsterdam was once home to the Dutch East India Trading Company: a company that was integral in transporting spices to Europe from across Asia. They also set up a number of spice plantations in southeast Asia, which are still prominent today. This punch celebrates the movement of these flavours.

1 vanilla bean
300 g (10½ oz) caster (superfine) sugar
50 g (1¾ oz) sultanas (golden raisins)
10 cloves
1 cinnamon stick
2 g (⅛ oz) whole nutmeg, grated
2 g (⅛ oz) black peppercorns, ground
10 g (¼ oz) black tea leaves
1 litre (34 fl oz/4 cups) genever
2 lemons, cut into wedges, to garnish

To prep Begin at least 1 month before serving. Halve the vanilla bean and scrape out the seeds. In a saucepan, combine the vanilla seeds and bean with the sugar, sultanas, cloves, cinnamon stick, nutmeg, black pepper and 500 ml (17 fl oz/2 cups) water. Simmer for 10 minutes over a low heat. Add the tea and simmer for a further 5 minutes. Strain and refrigerate. Once cold, combine with the genever and pour into to the barrel. Allow to sit for 1 month (see tip); there's no need to refrigerate it.

To serve Serve the punch directly from the barrel over an ice cube, then garnish with a lemon wedge.

Tip: Taste weekly, until it reaches your desired level of oakiness.

Small oak barrel with tap

Small whisky glasses

Winter

Fringe spider

Edinburgh Fringe Festlval takes place in August each year. It's a three-week-long festival of comedy, food and the arts. During festival time Edinburgh's population triples, with hostels and hotels booked out. Scotland's culinary delights are notoriously meaty and fried (often both at once), and the country is internationally renowned as the home of whisky.

small block of dark chocolate
300 ml (10 fl oz) Scotch whisky
300 ml (10 fl oz) mure
  (blackberry liqueur)
750 ml (25½ fl oz/3 cups)
  Irn-Bru
300 g (10½ oz) vanilla ice cream

To prep Begin at least 5 minutes before serving. Microplane the chocolate into a small, dry container, ready to serve.

To serve Combine the whisky and mure in a pitcher and top with Irn-Bru. To serve, pour the spider over scoops of ice cream in soda glasses, then garnish with the grated chocolate.

Tip: Drizzle mure over the ice cream for added decadence.

Pitcher

Soda glasses

Before going out to a comedy show

Tomato festival

 Watering can (make sure it's clean, with a spout)

Terracotta cups (think pot plants)

End of summer, when there is an abundance of ripe tomatoes around

No alcohol

In a town not far from Valencia, Spain, one of the world's largest food fights is held. Tourists converge on the streets of Buñol to engage in a huge end-of-summer tomato fight, purely for fun. Dump trucks fill the streets with tomatoes. Chaos ensues, with nothing escaping the tomato's bright-red stain. Fire trucks then hose down the town (the citric acid in the tomatoes actually leaves everything very clean) until the next year. Post-fight you might not be craving tomatoes for some time, but this punch is a delight made with the juiciest end-of-season tomatoes.

1 fennel bulb, roughly chopped
2 kg (4 lb 6 oz) beefsteak
    or similar large tomatoes,
    destemmed and
    roughly chopped
20 g (¾ oz) salt
100 g (3½ oz) honey
50 ml (1¾ fl oz) lemon juice
100 g (3½ oz) large green olives,
    to serve

To prep Begin at least 24 hours before serving. Remove the fennel fronds and refrigerate, ready for garnish later. In a food processor, roughly purée the fennel flesh, tomatoes and salt. Hang the mixture in a chinois suspended over a bowl overnight to allow the excess liquid to drain off. Set aside the solids (see tip) and refrigerate the tomato water, ready to serve.

To serve Combine the tomato water with the honey and lemon juice in a watering can, then top with ice. Garnish each cup with fennel fronds and serve alongside olives for snacking on.

Tip: The reserved tomato pulp from the tomato water makes a great base for a passata.

Good morning Ramazan

Istanbul is considered the city that connects the East with the West — a cultural hub that acts as a bridge between Europe and Asia. Ramazan (Ramadan) is the Islamic holy month, a time when people fast during daylight hours. There are also many religious celebrations during this month. In the early hours of the morning, drummers play to wake those sleeping for the morning feast, called Sahur. This punch adds sustenance to this meal to assist with the day's fast.

300 g (10½ oz) Medjool dates
200 g (7 oz) pistachio paste
   (see tips)
1 cucumber
10 ml (¼ fl oz) rose water
150 ml (5 fl oz) pomegranate
   juice
50 ml (1¾ fl oz) lemon juice
500 ml (17 fl oz/2 cups)
   sparkling apple juice

To prep Begin at least 3 hours before serving. Pit the dates and add to a saucepan with the pistachio paste and 1.5 litres (51 fl oz/6 cups) hot water. Simmer for 30 minutes over a low heat, then strain and refrigerate. Slice the cucumber into discs (see tips) and refrigerate.

To serve Pour the prepared date stock into a jug with the rose water. Add the pomegranate and lemon juices, then gently top with sparkling apple juice and the cucumber discs. Add ice to the jug to finish.

 Large stained-glass jug

 Stained-glass tea glasses

 Before dawn during Ramazan to give you sustenance for the day

No alcohol

Tips: Pistachio paste can be bought in specialty stores.

If you prefer, use a vegetable peeler to make cucumber ribbons instead of discs for an extra-fancy garnish.

Panettone Christmas

Vatican City is a city state inside the city of Rome, Italy, and the home of the Catholic Church. It's an historical city, moving to even the least religiously inclined. When we think of global religious holidays, Christmas is often one that brings families together. Panettone contains all the flavours of Christmas, and these sweet fruit loaves can be consumed alone, made into a pudding or even used to flavour your favourite alcohol for punch!

300 g (10½ oz) panettone
750 ml (25½ fl oz/3 cups) white wine
150 ml (5 fl oz) nocino
100 ml (3½ fl oz) grappa
750 ml (25½ fl oz/3 cups) Chinotto, to serve
100 g (3½ oz/⅔ cup) store-bought cinnamon almonds, to serve

To prep Begin at least 24 hours before serving. Blitz the panettone to a coarse crumb in a food processor. Combine with the white wine, nocino and grappa, and leave to soak in the fridge overnight. Strain slowly through a chinois – do not force it – and set aside the solids (see tip). Bottle into a wine bottle and refrigerate, ready to serve.

To serve Prepare the table with the bottle of panettone wine, a bottle of Chinotto, a bowl of ice and the cinnamon almonds for snacking on. Pour each drink to order at a 50:50 ratio over ice.

Tip: Reserve the alcohol-soaked panettone and mix it through bread and butter pudding for an extra kick.

 Wine bottle

Wine glasses

During Christmas feasts

Asia

Good fortune punch

 Fishbowl with a ladle

 Rice bowls

 Lunar New Year in the Northern Hemisphere, or when mandarins are at their best

Low alcohol

We had a great time developing this punch, trying to cram as many significantly 'lucky' ingredients into the bowl as we could and still making it taste good. It's designed to be drunk with friends during the Chinese/Lunar New Year festivities to ensure a prosperous year ahead. Mandarins are at the heart of this punch, as the fruit seems to take centre stage this time of year, often being given as a gift. Aperol (or a similar bitter red liqueur) colours the punch a lucky red, while orchids to garnish ensure fertility and abundance, and gold leaf, well, that symbolises gold and good fortune. One final note on luck: the punch should be served in a fishbowl. This is a nod to the final course of a traditional Chinese New Year meal, which is usually fish. Fish are said to represent surplus and wealth; the more fish you leave on your plate, the better your surplus and wealth for the year ahead.

100 g (3½ oz) caster (superfine) sugar
3 mandarins, peeled and segmented (reserve the peel)
15 g (½ oz) green tea leaves
5 g (⅛ oz) chamomile tea leaves
1 lemongrass stem, roughly chopped
30 g (1 oz) fresh ginger, peeled and grated
400 ml (13½ fl oz) Aperol (or a local red bitter liqueur)
sheet of gold foil, to garnish
stem of orchids, to garnish
200 ml (7 fl oz) verjus
8 fortune cookies, to serve

To prep Begin at least 12 hours before serving. Combine the sugar with 1 litre (34 fl oz/4 cups) water in a container and stir to dissolve. Add the mandarin peels, green tea, chamomile, lemongrass and ginger, then refrigerate. Combine the Aperol with the mandarin segments in another container and refrigerate. Allow to macerate for at least 12 hours. Slice the gold foil into long ribbons.

To serve Pick the orchid flowers. Strain the iced tea macerate into the fish bowl. Add the Aperol soak, including the mandarin segments. Add the verjus and top with ice. Garnish with the orchids and gold foil ribbons. Serve with fortune cookies.

Tip: For those wishing to abstain from alcohol, the iced tea component of this punch is quite the thirst quencher on its own. It's an adaptation of a welcome iced tea I developed for Future Future, a Japanese restaurant in Melbourne. All you need to do is omit the liquor and verjus.

Diwali sharbart

12 oranges
600 g (1 lb 5 oz) caster
  (superfine) sugar
50 g (1¾ oz) fresh turmeric root
10 green cardamom pods
10 saffron threads
15 ml (½ fl oz) rose water
50 ml (1¾ fl oz) pomegranate
  molasses
750 ml–1 litre (25½–34 fl oz/
  3–4 cups) almond milk
750 ml–1 litre (25½–34 fl oz/
  3–4 cups) lemonade
  (lemon soda)
750 ml–1 litre (25½–34 fl oz/
  3–4 cups) soda water
  (club soda)
bag of mixed nuts, to serve

Diwali, or the festival of lights, is a religious festival originating in India and celebrated by Hindus, Sikhs, Jains and even some Buddhists each year in October/November depending on the position of the moon. The festival goes for five days, which led us to develop a punch that can be enjoyed throughout the festivities.

A sharbart is a popular drink consumed on the Indian subcontinent. It's made with fruits or flowers and isn't dissimilar to a concentrated cordial in the western world. Here we have given you a recipe for the concentrate, which can then be enjoyed throughout the festival period with various mixers.

To prep Begin at least 4 hours before serving. Peel the oranges and combine the peels with the sugar in a container. Juice the oranges and refrigerate the juice, discarding the orange husks. Peel then grate the turmeric into the container with the orange peels and sugar. Bruise the cardamom pods by using the heel of your hand to press the flat side of a knife against them, then add the cardamom to the container along with the saffron. Place the container in a warm area until the sugar becomes fully wet, usually 2–3 hours. Add the rose water, pomegranate molasses and orange juice. Stir to combine and dissolve the sugar. Strain the liquid through a sieve into a cordial bottle, discarding the solids. Refrigerate until ready to use.

To serve Put the cordial bottle in the middle of the table with the almond milk, lemonade and soda water. Don't forget the nuts! Allow guests to mix a 50:50 blend of sharbart and one of the mixers.

Cordial bottle

Stained-glass teacups

During the festival of lights

No alcohol

Tip: If you have the time to make it, a black tea mixer is delightful with this sharbart. To make, just soak 50 g (1¾ oz) black tea leaves in cold water overnight in the fridge. The next day, strain it off and, hey presto, iced tea!

Bajigur for camping

100 g (3½ oz) palm sugar
400 ml (13½ fl oz) coconut milk
400 ml (13½ fl oz) Batavia Arrak
5 g (⅛ oz) ground ginger
2 g (⅛ oz) salt
dash of natural vanilla extract
15 g (½ oz) instant coffee
1 tablespoon smooth peanut
   butter
1 banana
1 cinnamon stick
¼ bunch of pandan leaves

 Billy can (camping pot)

 Jam jars

 In the middle of the bush
on a chilly evening, in place
of dessert

Low alcohol

When we looked at developing a punch for Indonesia, we knew it had to contain Arrak – of the Indonesian variety, of course. Batavia Arrak is a rum of sorts, distilled from sugarcane with fermented rice to help kickstart the ferment and give the product its wonderful funk. Be sure not to confuse this style of Arrak with those in the anise family (which wouldn't work in this punch), or Arrak made from the fermented sap of coconut flowers (which would work in this punch, but if you can get Batavia, go for it). Bajigur is quite popular in West Java, where it is consumed to help stimulate appetite, but our version is certainly more for post-dinner relaxation.

To prep Begin at least 1 hour before serving. Dissolve the palm sugar in 800 ml (27 fl oz) boiling water. Add the coconut milk, Arrak, ginger, salt, vanilla, coffee and peanut butter, then stir to combine. At this point you can transfer the mixture straight to the billy can or divide between six 250 ml (8½ fl oz/1 cup) jam jars for easier transportation.

To serve Peel then chop the banana and add it to the billy can along with the cinnamon stick. Add the contents of the jam jars to the billy can with six pandan leaves. Heat to just below boiling, then remove from the heat. Remove the cinnamon stick. Divide the punch between the jam jars, making sure each jar gets a pandan leaf.

Tip: Keep spoons handy to eat the bits of banana that don't come out of the jar.

Many plums in a top hat

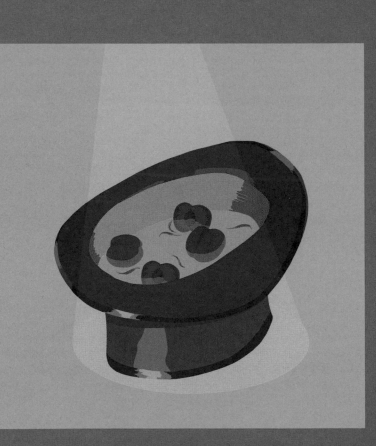

 Top hat lined with wax, with a ladle (see tips)

 Sake cups

When the weather's warm, the plums are ripe and the mood is whimsical

Low alcohol

They say the Wakayama region of Japan is the country's ume capital. While this punch pays homage to that place, it also pays homage to one of the greatest television shows of all time: *The Simpsons*. There is a scene where Moe the bartender is asked for 'a single plum floating in perfume served in a man's hat' by Yoko Ono, who later replicated this 'drink' for an art show. Umeshu is a Japanese plum liqueur. Naturally we have used umeshu as the starting point, with elderflower liqueur representing the 'perfume' and sencha tea giving a savoury balance. A tongue-in-cheek punch to enjoy in the warmer months when plums are at their sweetest.

15 g (½ oz) sencha tea leaves
5 ripe blood plums
350 ml (12 fl oz) umeshu
150 ml (5 fl oz) elderflower
    liqueur
½ bunch of tarragon
185–200 ml (6–7 fl oz) sparkling
    wine (about ¼ bottle)

To prep Begin at least 12 hours before serving. Combine the tea with 800 ml (27 fl oz) cold water in a container and refrigerate. Halve the plums. Add the plum halves and their stones to a separate container with the umeshu and elderflower liqueur, then refrigerate. Allow to macerate for 12 hours. Remove the stones from the plum soak and discard. Strain the tea into the plum soak and refrigerate until required. Prep the tarragon by picking the sprigs from the stems.

To serve Pour the prepared liquid (including the plum halves) into your serving vessel. Gently add the sparkling wine and slide in some ice. Garnish with tarragon sprigs.

Tips. If you can get your hands on pressed cherry blossom flowers, these make an excellent aromatic finishing touch.

We know lining a top hat with wax might be a bit ambitious, but this punch will be just as delicious served in a large bowl.

Mooncake punch

The mid autumn festival is quite popular in Singapore, with lanterns and mooncakes taking centre stage. These days there are many different types of mooncakes, so we opted to style our punch on the 'five kernel' mooncake, which uses five different nuts or seeds along with maltose.

1.4 litres (47 fl oz) almond milk
200 g (7 oz) maltose
1 tablespoon smooth peanut butter
1 tablespoon tahini
1 tablespoon chocolate hazelnut spread
5 g (⅛ oz) Chinese five-spice
bag of marshmallows
8 Anzac biscuits (or similar sweet oat biscuits), to serve

To prep Begin at least 1 hour before serving. Combine the almond milk, maltose, peanut butter, tahini and hazelnut spread in a saucepan. Gently heat and stir to combine, removing from the heat once everything is homogenised. Refrigerate until ready to serve.

To serve Gently heat the prepared punch to just before boiling. Pour into a thermos. Go look at lanterns. Pour the punch into glasses, dust with Chinese five-spice and plop in the marshmallows. It's especially good served with Anzac biscuits.

Tip: This drink can be taken cold quite nicely as well, which is probably your best bet if you are in Singapore, given the average temperature there. If drinking cold, I would omit the marshmallows or just eat them on the side.

 Thermos

 Latte glasses

Wandering the streets looking at lanterns during the mid autumn festival

 No alcohol

Gin, tea & tonic

6 Calamansi limes (see tip)
50 g (1¾ oz) caster (superfine)
  sugar
30 g (1 oz) Ceylon black
  tea leaves
1 Ceylon cinnamon stick
  (see tip)
tropical fruit of your choice
  (try to find something local
  and seasonal), to garnish
400 ml (13½ fl oz) gin
600 ml (20½ fl oz) tonic water

Porcelain punch bowl with
bamboo ladle

Fine china teacups

Warm autumn evenings when
Calamansi limes are at their best

The British considered Ceylon (present-day Sri Lanka) a colony from 1815 to 1948 and were instrumental in bringing tea to the island, which now produces some of the best black teas in the world; those from the Uva province are particularly good. Tea has been used in punch for centuries and is a popular ingredient for the 'weak' element in a recipe. Combine this with another British staple, the G&T, and it stands to reason that you'll have a positively dandy time.

To prep Begin at least 12 hours before serving. Zest the limes, adding the zest to a container with 500 ml (17 fl oz/2 cups) water. Put the limes in the fridge for juicing later. Add the sugar, tea and cinnamon to the container, then stir to dissolve the sugar. Refrigerate for 12 hours.

To serve Prepare the tropical fruit garnishes. Strain the tea soak into your serving bowl, discarding the solids. Squeeze in the lime juice, then add the gin and stir to combine. Gently top with tonic, then finish with ice. Garnish with the tropical fruits.

Tip: If you can't get a hold of Calamansi limes, you can substitute with regular limes: just use three and add an extra 20 g (¾ oz) sugar. Also make sure you check your cinnamon sticks; Ceylon cinnamon is desirable over cassia as it is altogether sweeter and subtler.

Full moon bucket

The Full Moon Party on Koh Phangan in Thailand is a must-do for the energetic wanderer. Held on the night of the full moon (funnily enough), you can expect concentrated Red Bull, cocktails in buckets, glow sticks, thumping music and an all-round good time – if you drink those buckets responsibly! Be warned, you will be cleaning sand out of your clothes for weeks afterwards.

350 ml (12 fl oz) white rum (see tip)
300 ml (10 fl oz) mango purée (see tip)
100 ml (3½ fl oz) coconut vinegar
½ bunch of mint
500 ml (17 fl oz/2 cups) Red Bull
250 ml (8½ fl oz/1 cup) soda water (club soda)
glow sticks, packet of sparklers and crazy straws, to serve

To prep Begin at least 1 hour before serving. Put the rum, mango and coconut vinegar in your bucket and stir to combine. Refrigerate until ready to serve. Prep the mint by picking the sprigs from the stems.

To serve Gently add the Red Bull and soda water to the rum mixture in your bucket. Top with ice. Crack glow sticks and add to the punch, along with the mint sprigs. Finish with sparklers and crazy straws. Light the sparklers and let them go out before taking your first sip, or you'll lose your eyebrows.

Tip: If you have fresh mangoes and want to get a bit creative, you can do so quite easily. Grab three mangoes, peel them and add the skins to the white rum overnight. Purée the flesh and set aside to use the following day.

Bucket

Straight from the bucket with crazy straws

During a full moon, ideally on the beach

Pho punch

 Saucepan or mini stockpot with a ladle

 Miso bowls

 When limes are in season

 Low alcohol

Pho is one of the great dishes of Vietnam, with the best of the best coming from Hanoi (in my humble opinion). It's a noodle soup with quintessential Vietnamese spices and broth that is boiled for days from various bones. The spices are easy to replicate in punch form, but not so much the rich umami flavour found in the broth. This led us to use coconut water and sake, which has a certain umami saltiness to it.

10 small red chillies
200 g (7 oz) caster (superfine)
   sugar
5 green cardamom pods
5 cloves
1 star anise
1 cinnamon stick
5 g (⅛ oz) salt
½ bunch of coriander (cilantro),
   to garnish
½ bunch of Thai basil, to garnish
3 limes (see tip)
400 ml (13½ fl oz) sake
400 ml (13½ fl oz) coconut water
400 ml (13½ fl oz) ginger beer

To prep Begin at least 3 hours before serving. Slice the chillies from the tips to just shy of the base, then repeat to make four 'flower leaves'. Put the chillies in iced water in the fridge for 3 hours. Combine the sugar, cardamom, cloves, star anise, cinnamon and salt with 400 ml (13½ fl oz) water in a saucepan. Bring to the boil, stirring to dissolve the sugar, then simmer for 15 minutes. Strain into a bowl and allow to cool. Prep the coriander and Thai basil by picking the sprigs from the stems.

To serve Juice the limes into your serving pot and set aside the lime husks for garnish. Add the prepared syrup, sake and coconut water, then stir to combine. Gently add the ginger beer and softly slide in some ice. Garnish with the chilli flowers, lime husks, coriander and basil.

Tip: If limes aren't in season where you are, you can substitute for oranges, which you should be able to get all year round in their different varieties. Just use two oranges instead of three limes and add 1 tablespoon apple-cider vinegar.

Oceania

Northern Rivers punch

Byron Bay is a beautiful part of the world, where fertile land connects the rainforest and the beach. This land is home to native citrus as well as one of Australia's most famous exports, the macadamia nut. The community there is known to favour all things natural and local. What better place for a refreshing afternoon drink to share between friends during the winter months? It's a time when tourists flock to the north in search of a warm winter break.

6 finger limes
½ bunch of mint, to garnish
400 ml (13½ fl oz) dark rum
400 ml (13½ fl oz) orange juice
300 ml (10 fl oz) nut milk
   (macadamia milk is ideal;
   see tip)
200 ml (7 fl oz) macadamia
   liqueur
100 ml (3½ fl oz) orange liqueur
100 g (31/2 oz) condensed milk

To prep Begin at least 30 minutes before serving. Prep the finger limes by slicing them in half and squeezing out the lime 'caviar'. Refrigerate, ready to serve. Keep the husks for garnish. Prep the mint by picking the sprigs from the stems.

To serve Combine the rum, orange juice, nut milk, macadamia liqueur, orange liqueur and lime caviar in a large jug with the condensed milk. Using a hand-held blender, give the mixture a good blitz to combine and froth up. Pour from the mixing jug into glasses filled with ice. Garnish with the finger lime husks and mint sprigs.

Tip: Make your own nut milk by blitzing 200 g (7 oz) nuts with 1 litre (34 fl oz/4 cups) water to form a pulp. Allow to sit for 30 minutes before straining through a piece of muslin (cheesecloth). The milk will keep in an airtight container in the fridge for up to 1 week.

Large mixing jug

An assortment of glasses from the guesthouse cupboard

A winter afternoon

Oval ball punch

The Australian Rules Football Grand Final is held on the final Saturday of September each year. It's a day that truly makes the city stop. A procession of 80,000 loyal fans walk along the Yarra River path towards the Melbourne Cricket Ground (MCG) to celebrate the culmination of the season. The sun may be shining, but the wind is still strong at that time of year, so a hot drink is a must.

6 black tea bags
150 g (5½ oz) honey
1 lemon
400 ml (13½ fl oz) grain whisky
4 oranges, to serve

To prep Begin at least 10 minutes before serving. Brew the tea in the thermos by adding the tea bags to 1 litre (34 fl oz/4 cups) boiling water. Allow to infuse for 3 minutes, then strain, discarding the tea bags. Add the honey and stir to dissolve. Slice the lemon into wheels and add to the tea, followed by the whisky. Put a lid on the thermos. Slice the oranges into wedges and pack into a picnic basket.

To serve Pour into thermos cups, in small amounts at a time so the drink stays warm. Enjoy with the orange.

Tip: This punch is also great with a meat pie or a sausage in bread.

 Thermos

Thermos cups

Quarter-time, half-time, three-quarter time; or just whenever you feel like it

Bula punch

500 ml (17 fl oz/2 cups) rum
  (see tip)
20 g (¾ oz) Korean ginseng
6 passionfruit
½ bunch of mint, to garnish
600 ml (20½ fl oz) ginger beer
400 ml (13½ fl oz) grapefruit
  juice

In 2014 an international poll proclaimed Fiji to be the happiest place on earth. The reason? Well, there are several. Not only is Fiji a tropical, sunny island, but its waters have a calming effect on visitors, and locals enjoy some of the best fresh food, much of which is grown on the island. Finally — and most importantly — there's kava. This root, a local favourite, is crushed and soaked in water to produce a ceremonial drink. It acts in a similar way to alcohol in that it has a sedating effect. Kava is not available everywhere in Fiji, but we think it sums up the happiness of island life, and we've tried to replicate that feeling with this drink. Don't forget to say 'bula' after every sip — it means 'life', and is traditionally said after each sip of kava.

To prep Begin at least 24 hours before serving. Combine the rum and ginseng and leave to sit for 24 hours. Strain, then bottle. Halve the passionfruit and scrape out the pulp. Refrigerate, ready to serve. Wash the husks and leave to dry out. Prep the mint by picking the sprigs from the stems.

To serve Combine the rum and passionfruit pulp in the mixing bowl, stirring to break up the fruit. Add the ginger beer and grapefruit juice, then top with ice. Garnish with the mint. Spoon the punch into the passionfruit husks to serve.

Tip: For a non-alcoholic bowl of happiness, replace the rum with sugarcane juice.

Large mixing bowl and serving spoon

Halved passionfruit husks

In the sun, while looking at water or dancing with friends

Honey punch

Located on the northern tip of New Zealand's South Island, Marlborough is known for its coastal walks and white wine, especially their internationally renowned sauvignon blanc. The area is also famous for its manuka honey, a monofloral honey from the nectar of the manuka tree. It is thought to have potent medicinal properties.

6 feijoas (see tips)
750 ml (25½ fl oz/3 cups) sauvignon blanc (see tips)
½ bunch of lavender, to garnish
½ bunch of sage
100 g (3½ oz) manuka honey
300 ml (10 fl oz) sparkling mineral water
200 ml (7 fl oz) gin

To prep Begin at least 4 hours before serving. Peel the feijoas and combine with the sauvignon blanc in a container. Leave to soak in the fridge for 3 hours. Strain and return to the fridge, ready to serve. Prep the lavender by trimming the stems to 5 cm (2 in). Prep the sage by picking the sprigs from the stems for garnish. Set aside the leaves you don't need for the garnish. Add the manuka to 200 ml (7 fl oz) hot water in a pot on the stove, stir to dissolve, add the left-over sage leaves and simmer for 5 minutes. Strain and refrigerate, ready to serve.

To serve Combine the honey water, fruit wine, sparkling mineral water and gin. Top with ice, then garnish with the lavender and sage.

Honey pot (Winnie the Pooh style)

Wine goblets

Autumn, when the feijoas are ripe and the wine is fresh

Tips: If you can't find feijoas, you could mix it up with kiwi fruit.

Other dry white wines would also work here, with a high-acid varietal like riesling being an ideal substitute.

Pavlova punch

The pavlova is a cake of meringue topped with cream and an elaborate offering of fresh fruit. It is popular in both Australia and New Zealand at Christmas and throughout the rest of summer. The origins of this dessert are hotly debated, with both countries claiming ownership. Either way, we love it, and we're not choosing sides. Instead, we made this mighty fine drink.

6 kiwi fruit
3 passionfruit
1 pack mini meringues, to serve
1.5 litres (51 fl oz/6 cups)
   strawberry milk (see tip)
2 egg whites
3 tablespoons malted milk
   powder

To prep Begin at least 15 minutes before serving. To prep the fruit, slice the kiwi into wedges and halve the passionfruit. Arrange on a plate with teaspoons and mini meringues.

To serve Combine the strawberry milk with the egg whites and malted milk powder. Add the passionfruit pulp and kiwi flesh and blitz using a blender or a hand-held blender to foam up. Pour into a milk bottle and serve with the meringues.

Tip: Make the strawberry milk yourself by combining 500 g (1 lb 2 oz) frozen strawberries with 200 g (7 oz) caster (superfine) sugar and 1.2 litres (41 fl oz) full-cream (whole) milk. Refrigerate for 24 hours before straining.

 Milk bottle

 Large milk glasses

Christmas morning

 No alcohol

Kau Kau punch

1 sweet potato
50 g (1¾ oz) brown sugar
50 g (1¾ oz) caster (superfine)
   sugar
2 limes
400 ml (13½ fl oz) shochu
   (see tips)
600 ml (20½ fl oz) ginger beer
100 g (3½ oz) coconut chips,
   to garnish
1 nutmeg, to garnish

Papua New Guinea is Australia's nearest neighbour. It's a country of tropical rainforest, where a lot of the population grows their own produce. Sweet potato, locally known as kau kau, is far and away the most important staple food crop in Papua New Guinea, with many families growing it themselves for the dinner table. A favourite way to cook kau kau is to bake it with coconut. All that fatty, starchy goodness was the inspiration for this punch.

To prep Begin at least 4 hours before serving. Cut the sweet potatoes into 2 cm (¾ in) cubes and roast in the oven at 200°C (400°F) for 30 minutes. In a saucepan, dissolve the sugars in 1 litre (34 fl oz/4 cups) water over a low heat. Add the roasted sweet potato and bring to the boil. Take off the heat, then blitz with a hand-held blender and strain through a fine-mesh sieve. Refrigerate until cool, ready to serve. Prep the limes by cutting them into wedges.

To serve Combine the sweet potato syrup with the shochu in your serving bowl and stir well. Gently top with ginger beer, then fill with ice. Squeeze in the lime and drop the wedges into the mixture. Garnish with the coconut chips and a grating of nutmeg.

Tips: We recommend shochu distilled from sweet potato.

Use large banana leaves to make sure the bowl doesn't leak.

A woven bowl lined with banana leaves (see tips)

Carved wooden cups

Trekking season,
April–November (not during
the wet season)

Polynesia punch

In Maori folklore Tiki was the first man created, with human-like wooden or ceramic carvings representing the stories or images of ancestors. These can be found throughout the Polynesian islands. Tiki design became prevalent in bar culture in 1930s America, and came to represent tropical escapism. To capture the idealised beaches and sunshine of the Pacific Islands, we couldn't look past Savai'i, the Samoan home of coconuts.

3 coconuts
400 ml (13½ fl oz) coconut milk
150 g (5½ oz) caster (superfine) sugar
3 bananas
50 ml (1¾ fl oz) lemon juice
6 taro leaves, to serve

To prep Begin at least 2 hours before serving. Carefully crack the coconuts in half with a hammer. Do this over a pan or jug to catch the coconut water. Reserve the coconut halves and refrigerate the coconut water, ready to serve. In a saucepan, combine the coconut milk with 200 ml (7 fl oz) water and the sugar. Peel, chop and add the bananas. Simmer for 30 minutes. Refrigerate, ready to serve.

To serve Add the reserved coconut water and the lemon juice to a saucepan with the banana mixture. Blitz using a hand-held blender, then add ice. Line each coconut half with a taro leaf and ladle in a scoop of the punch.

Tip: Once you're done with the punch, scrape out the white flesh from the coconuts, dry and serve in your next salad.

Saucepan and a ladle

Coconut halves

In the summertime

No alcohol

On a boat

The International Date Line runs through the Pacific Ocean, marking the point of each new day. Because of its geographical position, Kiritimati (Christmas Island) is one of the first places to ring in the New Year, with Baker Island being one of the last. Being less than 1000 km (621 miles) apart, it is conceivable that you could enjoy the New Year's festivities on one island, then catch a boat to the other and do it all again. With this much indulgence it is important to stay hydrated, which is why this recipe contains coconut water and mineral salts.

300 ml (10 fl oz) coconut water
5 g (⅛ oz) mineral salts
200 ml (7 fl oz) brandy
150 ml (5 fl oz) pineapple juice
100 ml (3½ fl oz) grenadine
750 ml (25½ fl oz/3 cups)
   sparkling wine
party hats and sparklers,
   to serve

To prep Begin at least 10 minutes before serving. Combine the coconut water and salts (see tip), and stir to dissolve.

To serve In a cocktail tin, combine the brandy and pineapple juice. Shake with a few ice cubes to froth up, then pour into the Champagne bucket. Add the coconut water and grenadine, stir to combine, then top with sparkling wine. Ladle into flutes and decorate with a party hat and sparkler. Toast to the new year.

Tip: The mineral salts and coconut water mix is to aid in post-indulgence recovery; make extra and refrigerate – it will come in handy in the morning.

Fancy Champagne bucket and ladle

Champagne flutes

New Year's Eve and New Year's Day

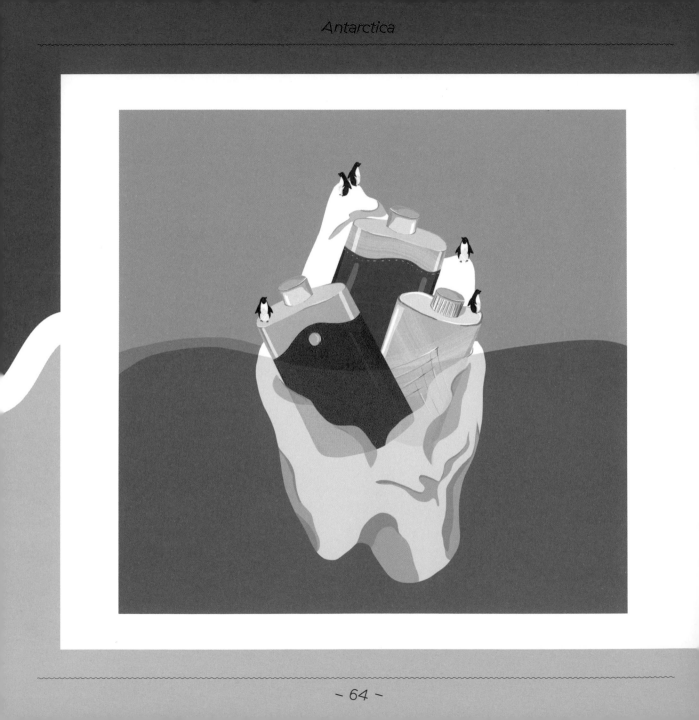

The world's coldest race

In the early 1900s the race was on to reach the southernmost point of the globe. The battle was between the British and the Norwegians, with the Norwegians claiming victory by a mere thirty-four days. This punch pays homage to that race using liquors that are popular in each nation, fortified with energy-giving coffee and milk powder, a must-have to ward off the cold.

150 g (5½ oz) brown sugar
30 g (1 oz) ground coffee
20 g (¾ oz) milk powder
1 teaspoon natural vanilla extract
350 ml (12 fl oz/1⅓ cups)
  Scotch whisky
350 ml (12 fl oz/1⅓ cups)
  aquavit

To prep Begin at least 2 hours before serving. Combine all the non-booze ingredients in a container with 800 ml (27 fl oz) hot water, stir to combine, then allow to cool. Strain off the solids and refrigerate the liquid until ready to use.

To serve Combine the milk mixture with the whisky and aquavit in your large flask and agitate to combine.

Tip: Be careful with this one; it's certainly not shy on the alcohol.

Large flask and a little funnel to pour into little flasks

Little flasks

 As Frank Loesser once wrote, when 'Baby, It's Cold Outside'

Hot piña colada

McMurdo station on Ross Island can house more than 1000 people doing various scientific studies. Given how cold it gets and the fact that fresh fruit would be a luxury, we developed this punch for all those scientists. It's something warming and familiar that whisks your mind away to a tropical beach and its hot rays of sunshine.

100 g (3½ oz) lemon curd
80 g (2¾ oz) brown sugar
50 g (1¾ oz) molasses
40 g (1½ oz) pineapple powder
   (see tip)
40 g (1½ oz) coconut milk
   powder (see tip)

To prep Begin at least 30 minutes before serving. Combine all the ingredients with 1.5 litres (51 fl oz/6 cups) water in a saucepan. Bring to just below boiling point, stirring constantly, then take off the heat.

To serve Fine strain the contents into a thermos while still hot, then dispense into mugs at leisure.

Tip: Pineapple powder is readily available online.

If you can't find coconut milk powder, you can substitute with regular milk powder. If doing this, substitute half of the plain water with coconut water to achieve that coconut flavour.

Thermos

Mugs

When you're cold and dreaming of warmer climes

No alcohol

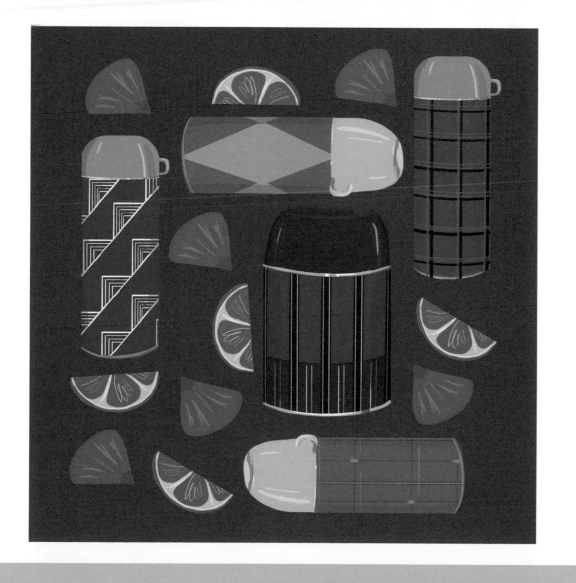

Africa

Mozzie swat

5 oranges
100 g (3½ oz) fresh ginger,
  peeled
200 ml (7 fl oz) apple-cider
  vinegar
100 g (3½ oz) caster (superfine)
  sugar
2 cinnamon sticks
small bunch of lemon balm
300 ml (10½ fl oz) Dubonnet
200 ml (7 fl oz) soda water
  (club soda)

Dubonnet is an aromatised wine bittered with cinchona bark that was originally created in the 1800s to persuade the French Foreign Legion to take their daily dose of quinine. At the time, North Africa was rife with malaria, but now Algeria has been considered malaria-free by the World Health Organisation. We've selected the ingredients in this punch for their health-giving properties: orange for vitamin C to boost immunity, cinnamon for its anti-inflammatory effects, and apple-cider vinegar for reducing fever.

To prep Begin at least 2 days before serving. Peel the oranges (see tip), reserving the peel, and roughly chop the ginger. To make the shrub, combine the peel, vinegar, sugar, ginger and cinnamon sticks in a sealable container with 200 ml (7 fl oz) water. Stir to dissolve. Refrigerate for 48 hours, then strain and refrigerate until ready to use. Pick the lemon balm sprigs from the stems and refrigerate until needed.

To serve Juice the peeled oranges and combine with the prepared shrub and Dubonnet in your fruit bowl. Top with soda water and ice, and garnish with the lemon balm.

Tip: Refrigerate the peeled oranges while waiting for the vinegar soak. This will keep them fresh for juicing.

 Ceramic fruit bowl with a mesh cloche and ladle

 Sealable sippy cups

 Whenever there is an abundance of mozzies

Low alcohol

Nyamuragira

 Volcano tiki bowl and ladle

Tiki cups

When things are getting tropical and you feel like letting off a bit of steam

The Nyamuragira Volcano in the Virunga Mountains in the Democratic Republic of Congo is the most active volcano in the world. The Volcano Bowl cocktail is a classic tiki punch, served in a bowl with a fiery centre. This punch takes inspiration from these tiki drinks and the smokiness of the volcano.

250 ml (8½ fl oz/1 cup) rum
250 ml (8½ fl oz/1 cup) brandy
25 g (1 oz) lapsang souchong
  tea leaves
bunch of mint, to garnish
punnet of strawberries,
  to garnish
300 ml (10 fl oz) orange juice
300 ml (10 fl oz) pineapple juice
200 ml (7 fl oz) orgeat
200 ml (7 fl oz) soda water
  (club soda)
100 g (3½ oz) fried plantain
  chips, to serve

To prep Begin at least 24 hours before serving. Combine the rum, brandy and lapsang souchong in a sealable container and refrigerate overnight. Strain and bottle until ready to serve. For garnish pick the mint sprigs from the stems and refrigerate until ready to serve. Hull and slice the strawberries and refrigerate.

To serve Combine the prepared spirits with the fruit juices and orgeat in your tiki bowl. Gently top with soda water and ice. Garnish with mint sprigs and strawberry slices. Serve with fried plantain chips.

Tip: Take this to the next level by using dry ice. *Do not* put it directly into the punch, but place in a bowl underneath and pour hot lapsang souchong tea over it. The result will be a delicious-smelling smoke.

The origins of beer

In ancient Egypt, fermented beverages were a part of everyday life. It is believed that the yeasts from bread making formed the base for the fermentation of the first ancient Egyptian beers. Today, modern brewers have revived a style of beer that emulates these libations, with flavours of bread and dates.

4 slices white bread
200 g (7 oz) caster (superfine)
    sugar
50 g (1¾ oz) Medjool dates,
    pitted
5 g (⅛ oz) salt
700 ml (23½ fl oz) beer (see tips)
100 ml (3½ fl oz) mead (see tips)
bag of buttered popcorn,
    to serve

To prep Begin at least 3 hours before serving. Combine the bread, sugar, dates, salt and 1 litre (34 fl oz/4 cups) water in a food processor. Blitz to a pulp, then transfer to a saucepan. Simmer over a low heat for 10 minutes. Pour through a chinois into a sealable container and allow it to drain slowly (do not force it). Refrigerate until ready to use.

To serve Make sure all the ingredients are cold. Pour the prepared syrup into your serving bowl. Gently add the beer and mead. Stir carefully to combine, then serve with popcorn on the side.

Tip: Any kind of wheat beer would be ideal here.

A lighter style (not heavily spiced) of mead will work best for this drink.

Earthenware bowl

Ceramic cups with handles so you can scoop the punch

 After a hard day's work

The home of coffee

Yirgacheffe is considered to be the birthplace of Arabica coffee (the variety that makes up roughly 75 per cent of the world's coffee) and, as such, the home of modern coffee. Cascara is the dried skin of the coffee fruit: a biproduct of the coffee bean harvest. This fruit lends a delicate tropical note to the drink, balanced by the bitterness of the tonic water.

1 pineapple (see tip)
40 g (1½ oz) coffee (roasted whole beans)
40 g (1½ oz) honey
6 g (2 oz) cascara
200 ml (7 fl oz) tonic water

To prep Begin at least 24 hours before serving. Wash and cut the skin off the pineapple. Put the skin in a container with the coffee, honey, cascara and 1.5 litres (51 fl oz/6 cups) water and refrigerate overnight. Strain, then refrigerate until ready to use. Cut the pineapple into wedges, ready for garnish.

To serve Pour the iced coffee mixture into your coffee jug and gently top with the tonic water. Pour into iced coffee cups and garnish with the pineapple slices.

Tip: For a more intense flavour, dehydrate the pineapple wedges in a very low oven (80°C/175°F) for 4 hours, turning every hour. Dehydrating them this way also means they will keep a lot longer. Store in an airtight container for up to 2 weeks.

Chemex coffee jug

Glass coffee cups

All day

No alcohol

WaTEAmelon time

 Watermelon

 Picnic cups

When you need to disguise drinking tequila at a picnic in the park

Kenya has a long history of tea production, with black tea being the major cash crop for the economy. More recently the government has been encouraging the propagation of watermelon due to the low set-up cost of watermelon farming combined with the high yield of the crop. Watermelons make one of the best natural punch bowls, so think before you chop into your next watermelon.

2 jalapeño chillies
400 ml (13½ fl oz) tequila
100 ml (3½ fl oz) agave syrup
20 g (¾ oz) black tea leaves
bunch of coriander (cilantro),
  to garnish
2 limes, to garnish
½ watermelon (see tip)
300 ml (10 fl oz) lemonade
  (lemon soda)

To prep Begin at least 24 hours before serving. Halve, deseed and roughly chop the chillies and combine with the tequila, agave syrup and black tea in a sealable container. Refrigerate overnight. Strain and bottle, ready to serve. Pick the coriander sprigs from the stems and slice the limes into wheels. Set both aside in the fridge until ready to use. Scrape the pink flesh out of the watermelon. Juice the flesh, ready to serve, and set aside the hollowed-out rind for the bowl.

To serve Combine 700 ml (23½ fl oz) watermelon juice and the spiced tequila in the hollowed-out watermelon. Gently top with lemonade and garnish with lime wheels and coriander sprigs.

Tip: You will have more than enough watermelon juice for this recipe, so pour the leftovers into an ice-cube tray and freeze, ready for your next gin and tonic.

Vase of vanilla

The Vanilla Coast, or the region of Sava in Madagascar, has long been known as the source of the world's best vanilla. Internationally demand for this delicious bean has continued to grow and, as a result, the price of vanilla has also increased over the years. However, this has not stopped it from being an integral ingredient in many foods and drinks around the world. The bean itself actually grows from an orchid, which is the reason this punch is served in a vase.

2 vanilla beans
450 ml (15 fl oz) rum
100 g (3½ oz) dried banana
   (not banana chips)
40 g (1½ oz) cacao nibs
1.1 litre (37 fl oz) bottle of
   cream soda
orchids, to garnish

To prep Begin at least 2 days before serving. Halve the vanilla beans and scrape out the seeds. Combine the seeds and beans with the rum in a sealable jar. Roughly chop the dried banana and add, with the cacao nibs, to the rum. Leave to macerate at room temperature for 48 hours. Strain the rum and bottle it, ready for use. Discard the solids.

To serve Pour the spiced rum into your serving vase and gently top with cream soda. Finish with ice and garnish each drink with an orchid stem.

Tip: Make a whole bottle of spiced rum at a time so that you are ready to go for the next gathering.

Vase and serving spoon

Glass teacups

On a humid summer evening.

Turmeric ramos

100 g (3½ oz) fresh turmeric root
300 g (10½ oz) caster
  (superfine) sugar
5 g (⅛ oz) salt
2 g (⅛ oz) ground white pepper
200 ml (7 fl oz) thick (double/
  heavy) cream
3 egg whites
5 ml (⅛ fl oz) orange-blossom
  water
20 g (¾ oz) dried rose petals,
  to garnish
soda water (club soda), to serve
  (optional; see tips)

Marrakesh is famous for its bazaar, full of vendors selling trinkets, fabrics and just about every spice imaginable. This punch takes inspiration from this mesmerising space. To capture its magic the punch had to be fancy, and there is no cocktail fancier than the Ramos gin fizz, a New Orleans classic that took more than ten minutes and half a dozen 'shaker boys' to make. We have combined the scents and flavours of the bazaar with the structure of a Ramos.

To prep Begin at least 3 hours before serving. Peel and grate the turmeric using a microplane (see tips). In a saucepan, combine the turmeric, sugar, salt, white pepper and 1.5 litres (51 fl oz/6 cups) water. Simmer over a low heat for 15 minutes, then strain and refrigerate until ready to use.

To serve In a bowl, combine the turmeric syrup with the cream, egg whites and orange blossom water. Very gently whisk to combine the ingredients. Pour half the contents (approximately 750 ml/25½ fl oz/3 cups) into a 1 litre (34 fl oz/4 cup) cream charger (see tips) and charge once. Shake for 1 minute. Siphon into glasses and repeat the process with the remaining prepared punch. Garnish each drink with dried rose petals.

Tips: Wear gloves when preparing the turmeric as it will stain your hands.

If you don't have a cream charger simply combine the ingredients in a shaker tin instead. Shake without ice, then shake with ice for as long as you can – 5 minutes ideally. Fine-strain into glasses and top with soda water.

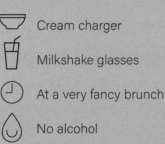

Cream charger

Milkshake glasses

At a very fancy brunch

No alcohol

Pinotage punch

In 1925 South Africa's now-signature wine grape variety was born. Pinotage is a cross between pinot noir and cinsaut. Not far from wine country is the home of rooibos, a leaf used to make tisanes, now recognised around the world as a tea. Another South African culinary contribution to the world food scene is biltong, or dried meat. This punch takes advantage of these local delights.

10 g (¼ oz) rooibos tea leaves
750 ml (25½ fl oz/3 cups) pinotage (see tip)
150 ml (5 fl oz) apricot brandy liqueur
100 ml (3½ fl oz) soda water (club soda)
2 apples, cut into slices or wedges
100 g (3½ oz) biltong, to serve

To prep Begin at least 4 hours before serving. Combine the rooibos with 500 ml (17 fl oz/2 cups) water in a sealable container. Refrigerate overnight. Strain and refrigerate until ready to use.

To serve Combine the pinotage, apricot brandy liqueur and iced rooibos in your decanter, then gently top with soda water. To serve, pour into wine glasses over ice and apple slices. Serve with biltong.

Tip: Select a pinotage that is on the lighter side.

Wine decanter

Wine glasses

Winter, while watching the rugby

South America

Fernet milkshake

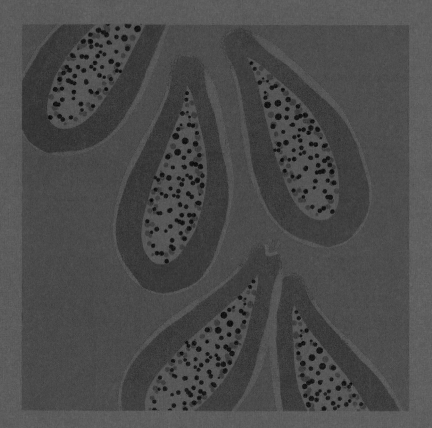

 Blender

 Milkshake glasses

 You can get papaya all year round, but there is a delicious glut in spring and autumn

With Spanish immigration to Argentina also came a favourite from their home country: Fernet Branca. This polarising drink is known for its intensely bitter palate, and the Branca family makes the most well-known version in the world. Blended with another South American favourite, dulce de leche (essentially caramelised condensed milk), this tipple makes for quite an intense but refreshing milkshake.

395 g (14 oz) condensed milk
½ papaya
½ bunch of mint (see tips)
750 ml (25½ fl oz/3 cups)
   full-cream (whole) milk
250 ml (8½ fl oz/1 cup)
   Fernet Branca

To prep Begin at least 4 hours before serving. To make the dulce de leche (see tips), remove the label from the condensed milk tin and place it, on its side, in a saucepan. Top with water until the tin is covered by at least 5 cm (2 in). Bring to the boil, then reduce the heat and simmer for 2 hours. Remove from the saucepan with tongs and allow to cool to room temperature before using.

Prep the papaya by halving it, scraping out the seeds and trimming off the skin. Segment into 2 cm (¾ in) cubes and refrigerate, ready to serve. For garnish pick the mint sprigs from the stems and refrigerate until ready to serve.

To serve Pulse all the ingredients in a blender until nice and smooth. This may take a while and a few scrapes of the blender to get the dulce de leche from the sides, as it can be quite sticky.

Tips: If you don't have time to make the dulce de leche yourself, it can be bought in a tin.

See if you can find chocolate mint; it's a delightful variety with hints of chocolate, which will serve this drink well.

Cascading chocolate punch

On the border of Brazil and Argentina is one of the most splendid sights the eye can behold: Iguazu Falls. Not the tallest waterfall in the world, but certainly the one that dumps the most water, attracting well over a million visitors each year. We thought the best way to pay homage to the falls was to create a punch delivered to its drinkers via a chocolate fountain.

1 kg (2 lb 3 oz) 70 per cent dark chocolate (see tip)
300 ml (10 fl oz) vegetable oil
200 ml (7 fl oz) overproof rum
100 ml (3½ fl oz) absinthe
40 ml (1¼ fl oz) aromatic bitters
punnet of strawberries, to serve

To prep Begin at least 1 hour before serving. Combine all the ingredients except the strawberries in a heatproof bowl suspended over a saucepan of simmering water. Stir until the chocolate has melted, then remove from the heat.

To serve Not all chocolate fountains work the same way, so please look at your user manual and follow that. The prep recipe gets you as far as having melted chocolate for the fountain. Serve with espresso cups (which guests can use to collect the falling punch) and saucers (to catch the mess). And, of course, no chocolate fountain would be complete without strawberries for dipping.

 Chocolate fountain

 Espresso cups and saucers

When you don't feel like a piña colada while getting caught in the rain…

 Low alcohol

Tip: The better quality chocolate you use the better the finished product, so don't skimp here!

Salty mocochinchi

 Wine bottles

 Enamel cups

As Shaggy once said, 'In the summertime when the weather is fine', which also happens to be when peaches are at their best. Perhaps the lyrics should have been 'In the summertime when the peaches are fine...'

Low alcohol

The salt flats of Bolivia are the largest in the world, and tourists flock to gaze in wonder and take funny photographs. Mocochinchi is a traditional Bolivian beverage that uses dried peaches boiled with sugar and cinnamon and is served chilled. This recipe takes inspiration from both with a punch that can be handily transported to the salt flats and consumed while it feels like you're floating on a cloud.

4 peaches (see tip)
750 ml (25½ fl oz/3 cups) dry white wine (clean and reserve the bottle for storing the mocochinchi)
300 g (10½ oz) caster (superfine) sugar
5 g (⅛ oz) salt
bag of pretzels, to serve

To prep Begin at least 24 hours before serving. Halve the peaches, removing the stones. Add the flesh to the wine and refrigerate overnight. Strain and bottle, ready to serve. For the mocochinchi, combine the peach stones, sugar, salt and 1 litre (34 fl oz/4 cups) water in a saucepan and bring to the boil. Simmer for 15 minutes, then strain and refrigerate, ready to serve.

To serve In a large bowl, stir together the prepared mocochinchi with the peach wine. Pour the liquid into the empty wine bottles. Pack them inside your daypack with some enamel cups for your long journey out to the flats. Or, if you are serving this at home, pop the bottles on the table with some pretzels and imbibe, dreaming of saltier times.

Tip: Stone fruit stones contain amygdalin, which, when ingested, is converted into cyanide in the body. We have tested this recipe and are still fine, but if you want to be extra cautious you can omit the peach stones.

Batida slushie

Millions of people flock to the colourful Carnival in Rio each year. It is held in February, traditionally to mark the beginning of Lent. Cachaça, a fermented and distilled spirit made from sugarcane juice, is popular at the festival and is Brazil's national beverage. A batida is a cocktail that blends Cachaça and fruit juice, sometimes condensed milk. Here we've gone for the best of both worlds and included a dairy element in the yoghurt, because why not? It's Carnival!

250 g (9 oz) panela (unrefined cane sugar)
6 passionfruit
500 ml (17 fl oz/2 cups) Cachaça
500 g (1 lb 2 oz/2 cups) natural yoghurt (see tip)
120 ml (4 fl oz) absinthe

To prep Begin at least 1 hour before serving. Combine the panela with 500 ml (17 fl oz/2 cups) hot water and stir to form a syrup. Refrigerate until ready to serve. Halve the passionfruit and scrape out the pulp, then refrigerate. Reserve six passionfruit husks for garnish.

To serve Combine the syrup, Cachaça, pulp and yoghurt in a blender and blend with crushed ice. Pulse briefly, then pour into margarita glasses and garnish with the reserved passionfruit husks. Pour 20 ml (¾ fl oz) absinthe into each husk and light on fire before giving to your guests. Tell them to allow it to burn out before pouring it into their drink.

Tip: Not all yoghurts are created equal, so make sure you use one with no added sugar, otherwise you'll be up all night on a sugar high.

Blender

Margarita glasses

When you're feelin' HOT, HOT, HOT!

Hydration punch

The Atacama Desert in Chile is incredibly beautiful and deserves a visit, but it is also one of the driest places on earth. It's so dry, in fact, that NASA has conducted similar testing to that performed on Mars to measure the capacity for the planet to support life. With a visit to such a dry place it is important to stay hydrated, so we've concocted the ultimate thirst-quenching punch. Even if you aren't heading to the desert, this drink will keep you well hydrated during your next summer party.

1 litre (34 fl oz/4 cups) coconut water
500 ml (17 fl oz/2 cups) aloe vera juice
100 g (3½ oz) caster (superfine) sugar
10 g (¼ oz) hibiscus tea leaves
5 g (⅛ oz) salt
2 lemons
1 cucumber

To prep Begin at least 2 hours before serving. Combine all the ingredients except the lemon and cucumber in a container. Stir to combine and leave to macerate in the fridge for 2 hours. Strain and refrigerate until ready to serve. Slice the lemons into wheels and the cucumber into discs and refrigerate, ready to serve.

To serve Pour the punch into a water dispenser, along with the lemon and cucumber. Place the dispenser on the table and allow guests to hydrate at their leisure. Serve with a bucket of ice and a scoop.

Mini water dispenser

Paper cups

When you are feeling defeated by the heat

No alcohol

Tip: This recipe loves to be scaled up and can be kept in the fridge quite conveniently for those hotter days when you aren't entertaining.

Flower festival punch

 2.5 litre (85 fl oz/10 cup) flower vase (relatively shallow and with a wide mouth)

Teacups, teaspoons and saucers

Springtime, or any time you're feeling a little floral

Low alcohol

The flower festival in Medellin started more than sixty years ago and has grown to become the most important festival for the town, with many events including a flower parade and a classic car show. This punch is a very floral one, with each ingredient prized for its alluring aroma. The really fun part is arranging the edible flowers. If you can't find the varieties listed, feel free to substitute with some of your favourite blooms. Just make sure they are edible and free from pesticides.

500 g (1 lb 2 oz) tinned lychees, drained and liquid reserved
variety of edible flowers (we like hibiscus, nasturtium, lavender and snapdragon), to garnish
600 ml (20½ fl oz) mandarin juice (see tip)
300 ml (10 fl oz) gin
200 ml (7 fl oz) elderflower liqueur

To prep Begin at least 10 minutes before serving. Strain the lychee syrup from the tin and set aside. Depending on your flowers you may want to trim them, ready to serve.

To serve Combine the mandarin juice, gin, elderflower liqueur and lychee syrup in a vase. Top with large blocks of ice. Arrange the flowers in the vase and serve with a bowl of lychees on the side. Instruct guests to serve themselves using the teacups and saucers to catch any drips. The teaspoons are there to enable respectable gorging on the lychees.

Tip: Fresh mandarin juice is a great elevator if they are in season locally.

Penguins & coconuts

3 young coconuts
3 limes
350 ml (12 fl oz) hydrosol
500 ml (17 fl oz/2 cups) ginger
  beer

Loved by ecologists for its unique environment and undisturbed fauna, the Galapagos are 97 per cent national park and certainly a sight to behold. Even the cold-loving penguins venture this far north to gaze at its beauty. Hydrosols, or non-alcoholic spirits, are becoming more and more readily available. There can be a lot of variety in flavours, so a taste test may be in order before choosing your favourite. The most famous brand is Seedlip, which has a few different varieties on the market. Their 'garden 108' would be perfect here.

To prep Begin at least 30 minutes before serving. Chop the tops off the coconuts (see tip) and drain and reserve the coconut water. Measure out 500 ml (17 fl oz/2 cups) coconut water and refrigerate, ready to serve. Drink the rest. Juice your limes and refrigerate the juice until ready to use.

To serve Combine the coconut water, hydrosol and lime juice in a large bowl, then divide evenly between the three coconuts. Pour 175 ml (6 fl oz) ginger beer into each. Gently top with ice and serve with straws. Drink directly from the coconut.

Tip: There are specialty coconut cutters on the market, which are inexpensive and will save some nasty cuts.

 Young coconuts

 Young coconuts and bamboo straws

After a long day when you want lots of flavour and refreshment

 No alcohol

Inti Raymi — Sunrise punch

There are reasons to head to Cusco other than catching a train to Machu Picchu, and Inti Raymi, or the Festival of the Sun, is one of them. Held on the winter solstice since Incan times, when they would parade mummies and sacrifice llamas, the festival has evolved to (luckily) not include such activities, but instead to praise the sun god through ceremony. This punch uses Pisco, a local favourite tipple, which is essentially an unaged brandy. Made in the form of a classic sunrise drink, this punch needs to be layered, so make sure you have a steady hand when assembling it.

100 ml (3½ fl oz) grenadine
250 ml (8½ fl oz/1 cup)
  guava juice
700 ml (23½ fl oz) orange juice
500 ml (17 fl oz/2 cups) Pisco

To prep There's nothing to prep for this recipe – just make sure all of your ingredients are cold, including the Pisco.

To serve Fill the carafe with ice. Gently layer (pour) the ingredients in the following order: grenadine, guava, orange juice and then the Pisco. Serve.

Tip: You could make these individually for each of your guests. Just follow the same process, pouring directly into the glasses (with adjusted measurements, of course).

Carafe

Small wine glasses

Winter solstice: dawn for the die-hards, dusk for the rest of us

North America

Crop over

The sugarcane harvest in Barbados honours the end of the season with a really big party: six weeks of festivities. With so much partying to do, we designed this punch to be non-alcoholic so that you can be sure to see the celebrations through 'til the end. However, much like the classic Caribbean cocktail Corn 'n' Oil — on which this punch is based — a splash of rum in there wouldn't offend.

20 g (¾ oz) blackstrap molasses
14 limes
800 ml (27 fl oz) sugarcane juice
200 ml (7 fl oz) falernum
  (see tip)

To prep Begin at least 1 hour before serving. Combine the blackstrap molasses in 100 ml (3½ fl oz) hot water and stir to dissolve. Refrigerate, ready to serve. Halve and juice the limes in a citrus press. You should end up with about 400 ml (13½ fl oz). Strain through a fine-mesh sieve and refrigerate, ready to serve.

To serve Combine all the ingredients in the oil can, pop the top on and give it a swirl to combine. Serve alongside a bucket of ice and thick plastic cups so people can help themselves.

Tip: Falernum, a lime, almond and pimento syrup, comes in many different forms. You can readily buy good versions these days, but it is also quite easy to make yourself, with many recipes available on the internet.

Oil can

Colourful, thick plastic cups

Spring is sugarcane harvest time, so get it while it's fresh

No alcohol

Maple apple toddy

 Small saucepan and ladle

 Enamel mugs

While ice fishing in Quebec; failing that, anytime there is snow around

No alcohol

Canada is famous for many things, from ice hockey to beautiful natural vistas, including the Canadian Rockies and the northern lights. One of the tastiest things to come out of Canada is, without doubt, maple syrup: the sap of a few varieties of maple trees, with most of it coming from Quebec. Starches in the tree are converted into sugars and then rise through the sap in late winter, when the trees are tapped for their sugary goodness. The sap is then boiled into the syrup we enjoy on our pancakes and in our punches.

½ cinnamon stick
10 cloves
5 green cardamom pods
10 allspice berries
1.2 litres (41 fl oz/4 cups) apple juice
150 ml (5 fl oz) maple syrup
100 g (3½ oz) salted butter
50 g (1¾ oz) custard powder
bag of marshmallows, to serve

To prep Begin at least 30 minutes before serving. Make a spice tea bag by combining all the spices in a piece of muslin (cheesecloth) and tying it up with twine.

To serve Combine all the ingredients, including the spice tea bag, in a small saucepan. Heat very gently for about 10 minutes, stirring frequently to ensure the mixture doesn't boil and everything is well combined. Once the butter has melted and the desired temperature has been reached, remove the spice tea bag and serve with marshmallows on sticks and a torch to toast them with.

Tip: If you want to booze it up, a splash of rum directly into your cup wouldn't be such a bad idea.

Pirates are jerks

3 teaspoons ground allspice
2 teaspoons dried thyme leaves
1 teaspoon cayenne pepper
½ teaspoon garlic powder
½ teaspoon onion powder
½ teaspoon salt
100 g (3½ oz) brown sugar
2 limes, to garnish
400 ml (13½ fl oz/1½ cups) rum
400 ml (13½ fl oz) pineapple
  juice (see tip)
500 ml (17 fl oz/2 cups)
  kombucha
small jar of preserved cherries,
  drained, to garnish
toy boat, to serve (optional)

Jamaica is famous for, among many other things, naughty pirates and delicious jerk seasonings. Allspice is the signature component of this spice blend, which is used to dry-rub meats before roasting to give them the Jamaican tang, as it were. If you haven't used it before, it is delightful. The name allspice actually came about because the English thought it contained all the properties of cinnamon, nutmeg and cloves, hence all of the spices.

To prep Begin at least 1 hour before serving. To make the jerk syrup, combine the spices, salt and sugar with 200 ml (7 fl oz) water in a microwavable container. Heat for 1 minute on high, then stir. Repeat twice more. Alternatively, warm in a saucepan over a low heat, stirring occasionally, for around 5 minutes. Strain through a fine-mesh sieve and refrigerate until needed. Slice the limes into wheels and reserve for garnish.

To serve Combine the rum with the pineapple juice and jerk syrup in your planter box, then gently add the kombucha. Garnish with lime wheels, preserved cherries and, if you're feeling nautical, a toy boat.

Tip: Make your own pineapple juice. Buy a large pineapple, juice half and reserve the other half for fancy decorations – and for eating, of course.

 Small barrel planter box lined with wax

Barrel mugs

When your buccaneers are hot and in need of refreshment

Horchata sorbet

 Bottle

Rocks glasses

When celebrating the life
of a loved one

 No alcohol

The Day of the Dead festival is a multi-day celebration of the lives of loved ones passed. Celebrated all over both North and South America, there is a particular focus in Mexico, especially in the Oaxaca region. A popular drink in this region is horchata, which is essentially a spiced rice or nut milk. This recipe is non-alcoholic, but it would work well with a variety of spirits. We suggest adding the favoured spirit of a passed loved one to celebrate their life. A single shot would suffice; just add it when you pour the horchata over the sorbet.

500 ml (17 fl oz/2 cups) almond milk
500 ml (17 fl oz/2 cups) rice milk
250 ml (8½ fl oz/1 cup) oat milk
250 ml (8½ fl oz/1 cup) coconut milk
100 g (3½ oz) agave syrup
50 g (1¾ oz) cacao nibs
1 cinnamon stick
2 teaspoons grated nutmeg
1 kg (2 lb 3 oz) tub of citrus sorbet (grapefruit works best, but any citrus will do; see tip)
bag of corn chips, to serve

To prep Begin at least 1 hour before serving. Combine all the ingredients, except the sorbet and corn chips, in a saucepan and gently heat for 30 minutes. Remove from the heat and strain through a fine-mesh sieve. Bottle and refrigerate until required.

To serve Prepare the table with the bottled horchata, citrus sorbet and corn chips. To serve, add a large scoop of sorbet to each glass and pour the horchata over the top until the sorbet is covered. Depending on the type of glassware used, measurements may vary, but 1 tablespoon of sorbet to 100 ml (3½ fl oz) horchata is a good starting point.

Tip: Making your own sorbet is easy and will certainly impress your guests – if done right, of course.

Peach the pony

The Kentucky Derby, potentially the most famous horse race in the world, is held on the first Saturday in May at Churchill Downs. This time of the year in the Northern Hemisphere is also when peach season is kicking off, and peaches marry oh so well with the spirit of the state, bourbon whiskey.

5 peaches
½ bunch of mint
300 g (10½ oz) caster (superfine) sugar
10 g (¼ oz) citric acid
750 ml (25½ fl oz/3 cups) bourbon whiskey
150 ml (5 fl oz) orgeat (see tip)

To prep Begin at least 24 hours before serving. Slice the peaches, remove the stones and grill the fruit in a hot chargrill pan for about 1 minute on each side, then set aside. Pick the mint sprigs from the stems, reserving half for garnish. Blanch the other half in boiling water for 10 seconds, then run under cold water to refresh. Combine the sugar and citric acid in a blender with 800 ml (27 fl oz) hot water and blitz to dissolve. Add the peaches and mint and blitz to a smooth consistency. Pour into ice-cube trays and freeze overnight.

To serve Depending on the size of your blender you will most likely need to do this in two stages, which is ideal as this will ensure the punch doesn't overheat and become watery. Combine half the bourbon with half the orgeat and half the ice cubes in a blender, blitz and serve immediately. Garnish each drink with mint sprigs. Repeat the process when you need to make the next batch.

Blender

Julep cups with metal straws

The start of summer through to the end of peach season

Tip: Making your own orgeat using different nuts can be fun too. Pistachio orgeat is delightful, but expensive to make. If you're keen, Google will show you how.

Tailgate punch

On January 15 1967 the first Super Bowl was held in LA. Since then the game has become a national phenomenon, with people coming from far and wide to enjoy it. A lot of those people would be tailgating, which is essentially grilling out and drinking in the car park before the game. We designed this punch with that in mind, using ingredients that would most likely make an appearance on Super Bowl day.

100 g (3½ oz) cheese puffs,
   such as Cheezels
100 g (3½ oz) caster (superfine)
   sugar
5 g (¼ oz) citric acid
700 ml (23½ fl oz) beer
400 ml (13½ fl oz) tomato juice
   (see tip)
200 ml (7 fl oz) mezcal
bottle of Tabasco
meat tray, to serve
jar of dill pickles, to serve

To prep Begin at least 1 hour before serving. Crush the cheese puffs in a saucepan with the sugar, citric acid and 300 ml (10 fl oz) water. Simmer gently for 15 minutes, stirring occasionally, then remove from the heat and strain through a fine-mesh sieve. Refrigerate until ready to use.

To serve Combine the beer, tomato juice, mezcal and cheese puff syrup in a small esky, stir to combine and spice with Tabasco to your desired level of heat. Ice it up, grill some meat and serve with dill pickles. Go team!

Tip: Making your own tomato juice is quite easy. Just blitz some tomatoes with salt and a bit of chilli, cook for 1 hour, then pass through a fine-mesh sieve. It certainly takes this punch to the next level.

Small esky (cooler) and a ladle

Cups with stubby holders (koozies)

Before the big game, any big game, even your granny's local lawn bowls championship

Cajun hurricane

Jug

Hurricane glasses

Mardi Gras in New Orleans, or any other time you are feeling colourful and festive

One of New Orleans' most famous drinks has been snubbed by bartenders for years, but if you break down the sum of its parts and use good-quality ingredients a hurricane cocktail can be quite delightful. We've opted for 'spicing' the rum with a Cajun spice blend that gives the punch an extra kick.

100 g (3½ oz) brown sugar
500 ml (17 fl oz/2 cups) rum
2 teaspoons smoked paprika
1 teaspoon cayenne pepper
1 teaspoon dried thyme
1 teaspoon dried oregano
6 passionfruit
½ bunch of mint
600 ml (20½ fl oz) orange juice
200 ml (7 fl oz) lemon juice
100 ml (3½ fl oz) absinthe
purple, green and gold beads
  for your guests

To prep Begin at least 24 hours before serving. Combine the brown sugar with 100 ml (3½ fl oz) hot water and stir to combine. Combine the rum with the smoked paprika, cayenne pepper, thyme and oregano. Add the sugar mixture to the rum mixture and allow to sit for 24 hours (see tip). Strain through a piece of muslin (cheesecloth) and bottle, ready for use. Halve the passionfruit. Scrape out the pulp and refrigerate, ready to serve. Wash and set aside the husks for garnish. Pick the mint for garnish and refrigerate.

To serve In a jug, combine the orange and lemon juices, passionfruit pulp and spiced rum, then stir to combine. Fill the hurricane glasses with ice and rest half the passionfruit husks, cut side up, on top like cups. Add 20 ml (¾ fl oz) absinthe to the passionfruit husks. Light the absinthe on fire and extinguish after the light show by pouring the punch mix over the top and into the glasses.

Tip: If you have a cream charger, you can rapid-infuse the spiced rum in around 10 minutes. Simply combine all the ingredients in a charger, charge with two bulbs, shake for 5 minutes, then repeat one more time. Strain the mixture and hey presto! Rapid-spiced rum.

Pumpkin pie punch

Harvest festivals happen throughout the world, but possibly the most well-known of these is American Thanksgiving, held on the fourth Thursday in November. Pumpkin is a Thanksgiving staple, which may be a bit surprising given prime pumpkin season is a couple of months before, but perhaps that is the exact reason for its popularity: it needs to be used up!

600 g (1 lb 5 oz) pumpkin
200 ml (7 fl oz) apple-cider vinegar
200 g (7 oz) caster (superfine) sugar
100 g (3½ oz) brown sugar
½ bunch of rosemary, to garnish
2 apples, sliced, to garnish
500 ml (17 fl oz/2 cups) dry sherry
250 ml (8½ fl oz/1 cup) pineapple juice
250 ml (8½ fl oz/1 cup) root beer

To prep Begin at least 6 hours before serving. Heat the oven to 180°C (350°F). To make the pumpkin shrub, peel the pumpkin, remove the seeds and dice into 4 cm (1½ in) cubes. Roast for 45 minutes, then remove and transfer to a food processor with 400 ml (13½ fl oz) hot water, the vinegar and both the sugars, and blitz until smooth. Pour into a saucepan and simmer gently for 15 minutes. Strain through a fine-mesh sieve, bottle and refrigerate until cool and ready to use. Pick the rosemary sprigs from the stems and refrigerate.

To serve Slice the apples into wheels. Combine the sherry, pumpkin shrub and pineapple juice in your Dutch oven. Gently add the root beer and top with ice. Garnish the top of the punch with sliced apples and sprigs of rosemary and pop the lid on. Serve at the table after dinner as an alternative to dessert.

 Dutch oven and a ladle

 Coloured glass goblets

 Late autumn to early winter, before the pumpkins start rotting in the fields

Low alcohol

Tip: You could also serve this in a hollowed-out pumpkin using the flesh gathered from the hollowing of said pumpkin. Just make sure you get the right type; some pumpkins are not conducive to carving and will result in the use of many bandaids.

Index

Thank you

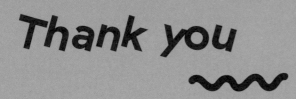

To our families, who cultivated our love for different cultures, and food and drinks alike, and who provided us with the opportunity to experience these wonders from a young age.

To our friends, who have been there through later adventures; there to share the nourishment and libations along our travels.

To the team at Hardie Grant: Jane, Loran, Jessica, Mietta, Astred and Andrea. The team that makes sense of our rambling ways.

To our business partners and colleagues at work, in particular Gilles, Lauren and Hugh. Thanks for your endless support. It means the world.

About the authors

~~~

Shaun Byrne and Nick Tesar have worked closely since meeting on the job at Melbourne's Gin Palace in 2013. In 2017, they founded Marionette Liqueurs, along with a couple of mates. It went on to win Champion Liqueur in the Distilled Spirits Awards in 2018 and 2019.

Shaun is an ideas man. After bartending, his first venture into production changed the game for a whole category: vermouth. Maidenii is now a mainstay in Australia's bars and, six years in, it's still innovating, with products winning titles such as Best Aperitif and Most Influential Spirits Innovation. Shaun's consultancy business, Good Measure, enables him to share his knowledge with the many start-ups that are entering the fold, and brings high-quality bars and local products to festivals across the country. Although you'll no longer find Shaun behind a bar, he's constantly powering away behind the scenes to produce and refine categories that others may have overlooked.

Nick never sits still. He is at the helm of some of Melbourne's most respected venues (Lûmé, Bar Liberty) and, while many peers are focused on gin or whisky, Nick is looking to the future of drinking. In 2019 he and Shaun published *All Day Cocktails*, a recipe book with a focus on no- and low-alcohol drinking. Nick continues to champion seasonality and the produce that is close to home.

Published in 2020 by Hardie Grant Books, an imprint of
Hardie Grant Publishing

Hardie Grant Books (Melbourne)
Building 1, 658 Church Street
Richmond, Victoria 3121

Hardie Grant Books (London)
5th & 6th Floors
52–54 Southwark Street
London SE1 1UN

hardiegrantbooks.com

A catalogue record for this
book is available from the
National Library of Australia

NATIONAL
LIBRARY
OF AUSTRALIA

Punch
ISBN 978 1 74379 607 8

10 9 8 7 6 5 4 3 2 1

Publishing Director: Jane Willson
Project Editor: Loran McDougall
Editor: Andrea O'Connor @ Asterisk & Octopus
Design Manager: Jessica Lowe
Designer/Production Coordinator: Mietta Yans
Illustrator: Astred Hicks, Design Cherry
Production Manager: Todd Rechner

Colour reproduction by Splitting Image Colour Studio
Printed in China by Leo Paper Products LTD.